中國古典愛情詩選

Treasury of

CHINESE

Love Poems

Bilingual Love Poems

中國古典愛情詩選

Treasury of CHINESE Love Poems

IN CHINESE AND ENGLISH

TRANSLATED AND EDITED BY
Qiu Xiaolong

Hippocrene Books, Inc.
New York

Book design and composition by Susan A. Ahlquist, East Hampton, NY.

For more information, address:
HIPPOCRENE BOOKS, INC.
171 Madison Avenue
New York, NY 10016

ISBN 0-7818-0968-1

Cataloging-in-Publication Data available from the Library of Congress.

Printed in the United States of America.

Table of Contents

Acknowledgments

Out of the treasury of the classical Chinese love poetry covering two thousand years, a small collection of about eighty poems cannot claim to be comprehensive.

It is nevertheless a project of love, for which I have enjoyed the generous help of many friends. I want to thank Professor Hegel, who has read through the whole text and written a most wonderful introduction, to thank Mona Van Duyn, whose clam chowder and poem celebrating the birth of my daughter has made it impossible for me to give up poetry, to thank Youzhen Su and Brenda Seale for their suggestions, and to thank a reader (whose name I did not catch in a reading at the Duff Cafe) whose memorization of the Chinese poems in *Death of a Red Heroine* prompted me into consideration of the project. Lijun has done the time-consuming job of typing the Chinese text, which I appreciate. And I am truly grateful to my editor Anne McBride for the pleasant and productive collaboration.

Introduction

For this introductory volume Qiu Xiaolong has chosen a number of well-known love poems from China's long literary history, in particular, the poems of the great Tang period (618–906), which have remained alive and on people's lips every since they were written. Most of the selection here date from that period; the rest were penned during the later dynasties, the Song, Yuan, Ming, and Qing.

With only a couple of exceptions, the poems here were written by men, although that may not be obvious from their content. This is because men frequently wrote in women's voices, because it was customary to do so. Why? In part, the female guise may have been chosen because it allowed men to express more "tender" emotions, personal feelings that might conflict with their official images as statesmen and administrators, as most of these poets were. Writing with borrowed voices also allowed poets to explore the experiences of others, especially the female entertainers who sang and danced, and provided more intimate services for them at their leisure. At certain times it was conventional to use women's voices, and love poetry,

1

to express a broad range of male desires, even political sentiments as well, such as frustration over lack of recognition for their accomplishments by their superiors. (This tradition dates back to the fourth century before the Common Era; it was originated by China's earliest named poet, Qu Yuan.)

If a poet writes of his longing for appreciation or for a friend (or lover) who is far away by using a borrowed persona, does that make his poem any less genuine, any less moving? I leave it to the reader to decide that, but I have never found poems of this sort to be so. A mark of these poets' success in ventriloquism might be seen by comparing them with poems written by women: theirs are not detectable in form, subject, imagery, or diction. As other good poets of their times, these women have followed common poetic practice in their writing. Only during the last four hundred years of imperial rule, after about 1500, did highly literate women in any number begin to correspond with each other in prose, and in verse, to create a women's literature with characteristics that distinguish it from writing by men.

Love poetry is one of several strains of the classical Chinese poetic tradition that originated soon after the beginning of the Common Era, during the

Han period (206 BCE–220 CE) and that continues still today. That is, writers of the 21st century can still compose poems in the *shi* form nearly two thousand years after it became popular. *Shi* poems have even numbers of lines, all of them having the same number of syllables (usually either five or seven) throughout the poem, and their even-numbered lines rhyme with each other. Many also quote or allude to earlier poems or historical figures as well. Writing in women's voices became even more pronounced in the *ci*, a second poetic form that developed during the Tang. Its origins are traced not to the educated males who served in government as with the *shi*, but to the songs of women entertainers. The entertainment quarter of the Tang capital Chang'an (modern day Xi'an) witnessed lively experimentation; melodies and musical instruments from Central Asia became widely popular. First singers composed new words in Chinese to fit these melodies, and then members of the literati followed suit. Many of the poems in this collection (identified by the name of the original tune that set the pattern of lines, numbers of syllables per line, and the rhyme scheme) are *ci* poems; even high ministers of state such as Ouyang Xiu relied on this vehicle to express powerful, as well as playful, emotions.

Surely Chinese is different from English in many regards; translation requires substantial rewriting, after all. The language of these poems was largely monosyllabic, with one written graph to represent each syllable. Dr. Qiu has wisely presented the originals of these poems facing his translations for the convenience of those who can read Chinese, and to inspire those who might wish to study the language after reading them.

But why should we read these poems, now seemingly so old and presented in an alien language? When Arthur Waley published his first collection of translations from the Chinese, they impressed a group of English poets and inspired the Imagist movement. They were seen as exotic, quaint, precedents for experimentation with new verse forms in English. Readers today are far more sophisticated about the world's literature than they were in 1919 when *One Hundred Seventy Poems from the Chinese* first appeared; that writers of other times and places could have the same feelings, aspirations, and fears as readers of English no longer seems so surprising as it was then. It takes little imagination to see ourselves in many of these poems, and the emotions expressed in the others are hardly incomprehensible, even when they may be unexpected. Qiu Xiaolong's selection presents love in many of its infinite stages and phases. Here we find young love, innocent and intoxicating, the aching longing of the married for their spouses, the fearful emptiness of couples separated by war, the joys of reunion, the anguish of the women left behind by men who probably never had any intention of returning. Some are clearly songs of a different time, when divorce was not available and women, constantly supervised by their families, could only be "virtuous" despite their wish to be otherwise. The images here are as haunting as they were to Ezra Pound's generation. They speak to us as they did to their original readers.

Qiu Xiaolong was initially educated in Western literatures in his native Shanghai. He took a position at the Shanghai Academy of Social Sciences as an expert in Eliot and Yeats, having won several prizes for his original poetry in Chinese. After coming over to the United States in 1988, he earned the Ph.D. in Chinese and Comparative Literature from Washington University in St. Louis in 1995. In this country he has won more writing prizes, initially for his poetry in English and more recently for his mystery novels set in China, also written in English. The latter have appeared in a

number of European languages as well as, most recently, in Japanese and Chinese translations. This is his first collection of translations of Chinese poetry. It is one of his purposes, as he has told me, to present a translation that, while faithful to the original in image as well as in meaning, will also prove to be as enjoyable to the reader here as is contemporary poetry written in English. Again, I leave it to the reader to decide whether he has achieved his goal. It is my view, however, that he brings to this project an extraordinary combination of scholarly understanding and poet's sensitivity to produce new renditions that are as vibrant as the original.

Of course the Chinese poetic tradition ranges broadly over a great range of topics beyond love. I hope that in a larger volume in the future Dr. Qiu may include some of those poems as well.

—Robert E. Hegel
Washington University
St. Louis

自君之出矣

張九齡（673-740）

自君之出矣，
不復理殘機。
思君如滿月，
夜夜減清輝。

Since You Left Home

ZHANG JIULING (673–740)

The half-woven cloth has hung
    untouched on the loom
since you left home.
Missing you, I am
like the fair moon
waning, night
after night.

望月懷遠

張九齡（673-740）

海上生明月，
天涯共此時。
情人怨遙夜，
竟夕起相思。
滅燭憐光滿，
披衣覺露滋。
不堪盈手贈，
還寢夢佳期。

Thinking of the Man Far Away in the Moonlight

ZHANG JIULING (673–740)

The moon rising above the sea
we share, far, far away
as you may find yourself.
Sad, sleepless, in the long night,
in separation, I think of you.
The moon so touchingly bright,
I extinguish the candle and step out,
my clothes wet by dew.
Alas, I cannot hold the moonlight
in my slender hand. I go back
into the room, perhaps
to dream again
of reunion.

長信怨

王昌齡　（698–757）

奉帚平明金殿開，
暫將團扇共徘徊。
玉顏不及寒鴉色，
猶帶昭陽日影來。

Deserted Imperial Concubine at Changxing

WANG CHANGLING (698–757)

At dawn, having swept the courtyard
with the broom, she has nothing else
to do, except to twirl,
and twirl the round silk fan
in her fingers. Exquisite as jade,
she cannot compete with the autumn crow flying
overhead, which still carries the warmth
from the Imperial Sun Palace.

閨怨

王昌齡（698-757）

閨中少婦不曾愁，
春日凝妝上翠樓。
忽見陌頭楊柳色，
悔教夫婿覓封侯。

Boudoir Sorrow

WANG CHANGLING (698–757)

Young, she doesn't know
how it is like to feel sorrowful
in her boudoir. In springtime,
gorgeously attired, she steps up
to the green balcony
to look out—

        The color
of the fresh willow shoots out there
precipitates her into regret:
She should not have sent him away,
so far away, going after fame.

相思

王維 (701–761)

紅豆生南國,
春來發幾枝?
願君多采擷,
此物最相思。

Red Love Peas

WANG WEI (701–761)

Oh, the *red love peas* that grow in the south!
There are a few, only a few
of them burgeoning in the spring.
Gather as many as you can, my Lord.
They are said to be most potent
in making you miss me.

長干行

李白（701-762）

妾髮初覆額，
折花門前劇。
郎騎竹馬來，
繞床弄青梅。
同居長干裏，
兩小無嫌猜。
十四爲君婦，
羞顏未嘗開。
低頭向暗壁，
千喚不一回。
十五始展眉，
願同塵與灰。
常存抱柱信，
豈上望夫臺！
十六君遠行，

Changgan Song

LI BAI (701–762)

With my hair first covering
my forehead, I plucked the flowers
in front of the door, and you came
on the bamboo horse, playing
green apricot catch
around the bed. Living
in the same Changgan Lane,
young, we were innocent.

At fourteen, I married you.
Still too shy, I hung my head low
to the wall and turned back
only at your repeated calls.
At fifteen, my face lit up
in your company, I was willing
to have my ashes mixed with yours.
You were as faithful
as the legendary lover standing steady

瞿唐灩澦堆。
五月不可觸，
猿聲天上哀。
門前舊行迹，
一一生綠苔。
苔深不能掃，
落葉秋風早。
八月蝴蝶黃，
雙飛西園草。
感此傷妾心，
坐愁紅顏老。
早晚下三巴，
預將書報家。
相迎不道遠，
直至長風沙。

against with the rising tide. Little did I think
I would mount the Husband-Watching-Plateau.

At sixteen, you traveled far away,
sailing across the Qutang Gorge,
the Yanyuan Rocks jutting out
so dangerously in the summer
and monkeys crying sadly
in the high mountains.
The footprints you left, step
by step, by our door, were moss-covered,
the moss too deep
to be swept away, leaves falling
in the early autumn wind.

Now the butterflies, yellow
in September, fly in pairs
over the grass in the west garden.
The scene breaks my heart.
I grow old worrying about you.
Oh when you are coming back
through the Three Gorges, write a letter home.
I will come out to meet you
as far as Changfengsha.

玉階怨

李白（701–762）

玉階生白露，
夜久侵羅襪。
却下水晶簾，
玲瓏望秋月。

22

An Imperial Concubine Waiting at Night

Li Bai (701–762)

Waiting, she finds her silk stockings
soaked with the dew drops
glistening on the marble palace steps.
Finally, she is moving
to let the crystal-woven curtain fall
when she casts one more glance
at the glamorous autumn moon.

月夜

杜甫（712-770）

今夜鄜州月，
閨中只獨看。
遙憐小兒女，
未解憶長安。
香霧雲鬟濕，
清輝玉臂寒。
何時倚虛幌，
雙照淚痕干。

The Bright Moon Night*

DU FU (712–770)

Tonight, in your boudoir, alone,
you are watching the moon
shining over Fuzhou City,
our poor children still too young
to share your longing
for me far, far away in Chang'an:
your long hair, cloud-like, wet
with the sweet night mist,
your bare, jade-smooth arms cold
in the clear moonlight.
Oh, when can we stand leaning against each
other, against the curtain drawn aside,
letting the moonlight dry the tears
on our both faces?

*In 756, Du Fu ran away with his family from the capital Chang'an to
Fuzhou because of An Lushan's rebellion, but Du was captured and
escorted to Chang'an, where he wrote this poem, thinking of his wife.

25

春怨

劉方平（742?-779?）

紗窗日落漸黃昏，
金屋無人見淚痕。
寂寞空庭春欲曉，
梨花滿地不開門。

Spring Grief

Liu Fangping (742?–779?)

The sun setting against the gauze curtain,

the dusk is drawing nearer

when she sheds tears, alone,

in her magnificent room.

The courtyard appears so deserted,

the spring on the decline,

pear petals fallen all over the ground—

too much for her

to push open the door.

玉臺體

權德輿（759-818）

昨夜裙帶解，
今朝蟢子飛。
鉛華不可弃，
莫是藁砧歸。

Happy Spider

Quan Deyu (759–818)

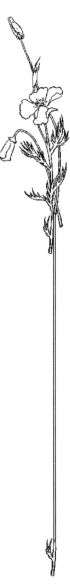

Last night, I saw my girdle unfurled
by itself. This morning, I see
a Happy Spider dangling
ecstatically, as if it had wings.
Signs of his finally coming
back home? I hasten
to put a finishing touch
to my make-up.

望夫石

王建　(766-830?)

望夫處, 江悠悠.
化爲石, 不回頭。
山頭日日風復雨,
行人歸來石應語。

Husband-Watching Rock

Wang Jian (766–830?)

Where she stood looking out for her husband,
the water of the river flowed on
to the horizon. Now
she's turned into a rock, which
continues to look out
without ever turning back, day in,
day out, against the wind and rain
on the hill . . .

When he comes back,
the rock should speak out.

題都城南莊

崔護（790年間）

去年今日此門中，
人面桃花相映紅。
人面不知何處去，
桃花依舊笑春風。

Lines on South Village

CUI HU (AROUND 790)

This door, this day, last year,
you blushed,
the blushing faces
of the peach blossoms reflecting
yours.

This door, this day,
this year, where are you,
the peach blossoms still giggling
at the spring breeze?

節婦吟

張籍 (?-830)

君知妾有夫，
贈妾雙明珠，
感君纏綿意，
系在紅羅襦。
妾家高樓連苑起，
良人執戟明光裏。

知君用心如日月，
事夫誓擬同生死。
還君明珠雙淚垂，
何不相逢未嫁時。

A Virtuous Wife

Zhang Ji (?-d. 830)

Knowing I am married, you gave me
a pair of lustrous pearls.
Beholden to you for your kindness,
I fastened them to my red slip.

My house is close to the Mingguang Palace,
where my husband serves as a guard.

Your intention is as lofty
as the sun and the moon, I know.
Having sworn to be with him
in life and death, I have
to return the glistening pearls to you
with tears in my eyes.
Oh, if we could have met
before I married.

春怨

金昌緒(850年間)

打起黄鶯兒，
莫教枝上啼。
啼時驚妾夢，
不得到遼西。

Spring Sorrow

JIN CHANGXU (AROUND 850)

Oh drive those orioles far, far away!
Don't let them warble
on that tree. When they do,
I awake from my dream
of going to the man who battles
on the northern frontiers.

隴西行

陳陶 (812-855)

誓掃匈奴不顧身，
五千貂錦喪胡塵。
可憐無定河邊骨，
猶是春閨夢裏人。

By the Wuding River

CHEN TAO (812–855)

Pledged to wipe out the Huns,
they fought without a thought
for themselves, and died,
all of them, five thousand sable-clad warriors,
lost in the dust of North.
Alas, the white bones by the Wuding River
still come to haunt her spring dreams,
in the shape of her man.

贈別

杜牧 (803-852)

娉娉裊裊十三余，
豆蔻梢頭二月初。
春風十裏揚州路，
卷上珠簾總不如。

Parting

DU MU (803–852)

Slender, supple, she's just thirteen,
the tip of a cardamom bud
in early spring.
Miles and miles along Yangzhou Road,
the spring wind keeps flapping up
one pearl-woven curtain
after another, behind which
no one matches her.

贈別

杜牧 (803-852)

多情却是總無情，
惟覺樽前笑不成。
蠟燭有心還惜別，
替人垂淚到天明。

Parting (2)

Du Mu (803–852)

Too much passion appears, inevitably,
to be too little.
Over the cups, I despair
of bringing up a smile.
The candle has its wick trembling like a heart
sympathizing with our parting,
and shedding its tears for us,
till the break of the day.

瑶琴怨

温庭筠 (812-870)

冰簟銀床夢不成，
碧天如水夜雲輕。
雁聲遠過蕭湘去，
十二樓中月自明。

Lament of the Inlaid Lute

Wen Tingyun (812–870)

Still, no dream comes to her,
the split-bamboo-made mat cool
on the silver-inlaid bed.
The deep blue skies appear like water,
the night clouds insubstantial.
The cries of the wild geese journey
as far as the Xiaoxiang River.
The moon continues to shine
bright into her tower room.

菩薩蠻

温庭筠 (812-870)

玉樓明月長相憶，
柳絲裊娜春無力。
門外草萋萋，
送君聞馬嘶。

畫羅金翡翠，
香燭銷成淚。
花落子規啼，
綠窗殘夢迷。

A Green-Shaded Window

(To the tune of Pusaman)

WEN TINGYUN (812–870)

The bright moon, the jade room—
the long memories . . .
The willow shoots swing so softly
in the languid spring breeze.
The weeds grown high beyond our gate
obliterated your departing figure,
but not your horse's neigh.

Against the satin valance
painted with flying golden kingfishers,
a perfumed candle dissolves in tears.
Amid withering flowers and weeping cuckoos,
appears a green-shaded window,
still lost in dream.

更漏子

温庭筠(812–870)

柳絲長,
春雨細,
花外漏聲迢遞。
驚塞雁,
起城烏,
畫屏金鷓鴣。

香霧薄,
透簾幕,
惆悵謝家池閣。
紅燭背,
繡簾垂,
夢長君不知。

Water-Hourglass

(To the tune of Genglouzi)

WEN TINGYUN (812–870)

The willow shoots long, the spring rain light,
beyond the flowers, the water-hourglass
drips, distantly,
flushing the wild geese at the frontier
and the birds on the city wall,
but not the golden partridge painted on the screen.

The thin mist of the incense comes
through the embroidered curtain.
Overlooking the pond, her room is wrapped in solitude
Against a red candle,
behind the brocade valence hung low,
her dream is long, unknown to him.

夢江南

温庭筠 (812-870)

梳洗罷，
獨倚望江樓。
過盡千帆皆不是，
斜輝脈脈水悠悠。
腸斷白蘋洲。

The Islet Enclosed in White Duckweed

(To the tune of Meng Jiangnan)

WEN TINGYUN (812–870)

After applying her make-up,
she stands leaning against the balcony,
alone, looking out to the river,
to thousands of sails passing along—
none is the one she waits for.
The sun setting slant,
the water running silent into the distance.
Her heart breaks
at the sight of the islet enclosed
in white duckweed.

無題

李商隱(813-858)

相見時難別亦難，
東風無力百花殘。
春蠶到死絲方盡，
蠟炬成灰淚始干。
曉鏡但愁雲鬢改，
夜吟應覺月光寒。
蓬萊此去無多路，
青鳥殷勤為探看。

Untitled

LI SHANGYIN (813–859)

It is hard to meet,
but hard to part too,
the east wind languid, hundreds of flowers wasted.
A spring silkworm may not stop spinning
silk until death. A candle's tears dry
only when it is burned down to ashes.

In the morning's bronze mirror, you worry
about the change in your hair,
and you feel the moonlight cold,
reading alone in the night.

Mount Penglai, so celebrated in fairy tales,
cannot be located far away:
O Bluebird, please go there kindly,
and take a look for me.

夜雨寄北

李商隱 (813–858)

君問歸期未有期，
巴山夜雨漲秋池。
何當共剪西窗燭，
却話巴山夜雨時。

Letter to the North in the Night Rain

LI SHANGYIN (813–858)

When can you come back?
Alas, I have no answer to give.
Here, the autumn pool is swelling
with the rain on Mount Ba
deep in the night.
                    Oh when
can we reach out again
in one move
to trim the candle by the western window,
and talk about the moment
of the rain falling,
falling deep in the night
on Mount Ba?

錦瑟

李商隱 (813-858)

錦瑟無端五十弦，
一弦一柱思華年。
莊生曉夢迷蝴蝶，
望帝春心托杜鵑。
滄海月明珠有泪，
藍田日暖玉生烟。
此情可待成追憶，
只是當時已惘然。

Decorated Zither

Li Shangyin (813–858)

A decorated zither, for no reason, is made
of fifty strings—one string, one peg,
each reminiscent of the youthful years . . .
Waking in the morning, Master Zhuang wonders
whether he dreams of being a butterfly,
or a butterfly dreams of being Master Zhuang.
Wangdi, an ancient emperor, poured out his grief
into the cuckoo cries in the spring.
A pearl holds its tears
against the bright moon on the blue ocean;
a jade-induced mist arises under the warm sun
over Liantian field . . .
Oh, this feeling, to be recollected later
in memories, is already confused.

贈內人

張祜(?–859)

禁門宮樹月痕過，
媚眼微看宿鷺窠。
斜拔玉釵燈影畔，
剔開紅焰救飛蛾。

To a Palace Lady

ZHANG HU (?–859?)

The moon moving beyond the trees
in the palace courtyard,
the egrets returning
to their nest in her lambent eyes,
under the lamp shadow,
she snatches out a jade hairpin
to save a struggling moth
by cutting through the red flame.

女冠子

韋莊(836–910)

昨夜夜半，
枕上分明夢見。
語多時，
依舊桃花面，
頻低柳葉眉。

半羞還半喜，
欲去又依依。
覺來知是夢，
不勝悲。

Last Night

(*To the tune of Nüguanzi*)

WEI ZHUANG (836–910)

In the depths of last night
I saw you in the dream.
We murmured on and on—
your face flushing again like a peach blossom,
your eyebrows arching like long graceful willow leaves.

Half shy, half ecstatic,
you tarried at parting—

                Waking up

overwhelms me in sadness.

應天長

韋莊 (836-910)

別來半歲音書絶,
一寸離腸千萬結。
難相見, 易相別,
又是玉樓花似雪。

暗相思, 無處說,
惆悵夜來烟月。
想得此時情切,
泪沾紅袖黦。

Thousands of Knots at Heart

(To the tune of Yingtianchang)

WEI ZHUANG (836–910)

No letter has come from you
for half a year: One inch
of separation grief,
thousands of knots in the heart.
It's easy to part, but not easy
to meet. Again,
the jade abode is covered
in the willow catkins like snow.

There's no describing how I miss you.
Melancholy comes with the mist and the moon
in the evening. Overwhelmed
at the thought of you, I raise
my red sleeves soaked in tears.

江陵愁望寄子安

魚玄機 (844?-871?)

楓葉千枝復萬枝，
江橋掩映暮帆遲。
憶君心似西江水，
日夜東流無歇時。

Look out from the Riverside

YU XUANJI (844?–871?)

Myriads of maple leaves
upon myriads of maple leaves
silhouetted against the bridge,
a few sails return late in the dusk.

How do I miss you?

My thoughts run like
the water in the West River,
flowing eastward, never-ending,
day and night.

菩薩蠻

牛嶠(859-920)

玉爐冰簟鴛鴦錦,
粉融香汗流山枕。
簾外轆轤聲,
斂眉含笑驚。

柳陰烟漠漠,
低鬟蟬釵落。
須作一生拼,
盡君今日歡。

The Incense Burning

(*To the tune of Pusaman*)

NIU QIAO (850–920)

The incense burning, burning, burning
in the jade container,
I throw aside the satin quilt embroidered
with a pair of mandarin ducks
on the woven-split-bamboo mat,
the sweat-melt powder dripping
on a hill-shaped pillow.
Out the window, the sudden sound
of the approaching wheels
flushes a smile against my knitted brows.

The willow shoots are looming up through the mist.
I find my hair disheveled,
the cicada-shaped hairpin dropped to the ground.
What worries should I have
about the days to come
as long as you enjoy me to the full today?

生查子

牛希濟(?-925?)

春山烟欲收,
天淡星稀小。
殘月臉邊明,
別泪臨清曉。

語已多, 情未了。
回首猶重道:
記得綠羅裙,
處處憐芳草。

Green Skirt

(To the tune of Shengchazi)

NIU XIJI (?–925?)

The mist is disappearing
around the spring mountains,
the stars so few, little,
against the bleached skies.
The sinking moon illuminates your face.
The dawn glistens in your clear tears
at parting.

A whole night's talk is not long enough
for all we have in our hearts.
Turning, you repeat:
Remember my green skirt, everywhere,
everywhere, you step over the grass so lightly.

鵲踏枝

馮延巳(903-960)

庭院深深深幾許?
楊柳堆烟,
簾幕無重數。
玉勒雕鞍游冶處,
樓高不見章臺路。

雨橫風狂三月暮,
門掩黃昏,
無計留春住。
泪眼問花花不語,
亂紅飛過秋千去。

Deep Courtyard
(*To the tune of Quetazhi*)
FENG YANSI (903–960)

Deep, deep is the courtyard.
How deep? Willows surrounding,
curtains upon curtains, too many
to count.
      There,
he pulls up the magnificent carriage
by the courtesan quarters. Here,
I mount the tower, unable to see him
on the road of pleasure.

The wind and rain rage in late April.
The door closes in the dusk.
There is no way of holding the spring.
Tearfully, I ask the flowers,
who do not answer,
in a riot of red falling over the swing.

蝶戀花

馮延巳 (903-960)

幾日行雲何處去？
忘了歸來，
不道春將暮。
百草千花寒食路，
香車系在誰家樹？

泪眼倚樓頻獨語。
雙燕來時，
陌上相逢否？
繚亂春愁如柳絮，
悠悠夢裏無尋處。

A Cloud in Travel

(To the tune of Dielianhua)

FENG YANSI (903–960)

So many days, where have you been—
like a traveling cloud
that forgets to come back,
unaware of the spring drawing to an end?
Flowers and weeds spread untrammeled along the road
on the Cold-Food Day.
Your scented coach is
tethered to a tree—
by whose gate?

Tears brimming in my eyes,
I lean on the balcony, alone,
to query a pair of returning swallows:
Have you seen him on the path?
Spring sorrow flutters like willow catkin.
I fail to find you even in a dream.

謁金門

馮延巳 (903-960)

風乍起,
吹皺一池春水。
閑引鴛鴦香徑裏,
手揉紅杏蕊。

鬥鴨闌干遍倚,
碧玉搔頭斜墜。
終日望君君不至,
舉頭聞鵲喜。

Pool of Spring Water
(To the tune of Yejinmen)

FEN YANSI (903–960)

The wind springs up,
rumpling a pool of spring water.
Along the fragrant trail, she teases
a pair of mandarin ducks,
crushing red apricot petals in her hand.

Watching the frolicking ducks,
she long leans against the rail,
her green jade hairpin trembling,
about to fall. All day she aches
for his sight, in vain.
Unexpectedly, she raises her head
at the sound of magpies.

寄人

張泌(930-?)

別夢依依到謝家，
小廊回合曲闌斜。
多情只有春庭月，
猶爲離人照落花。

To Someone

ZHANG MI (930–?)

After parting, the lingering dream
keeps returning to the old scene:
The small verandah surrounds
with the winding balustrade.
There is only the spring moon
that remains sympathetic, still shining
for a lonely visitor, reflecting
on the petals fallen
in a deserted courtyard.

浣溪沙

李璟(916-961)

菡萏香消翠葉殘，
西風愁起碧波間。
還與韶光共憔悴，
不堪看。

細雨夢回鷄塞遠，
小樓吹徹玉笙寒。
多少淚珠何限恨，
倚闌干。

The Jade Flute
(*To the tune of Huanxisha*)
LI JING (916–961)

The lotus blossom losing its aroma
and its leaves fading in verdancy,
the west wind sighing and vexing
the green ripples,
it is unbearable to see
the beauty ravaged by time.

In a drizzle, a dream returns
to the far-away frontier.
A melody keeps arising out of the tiny tower
until the jade flute turns too cold
for the player to continue.
How many pearls of tears,
how much anguish
in her heart, she leans, alone,
against the balustrade.

清平樂

李煜(937-978)

別來春半，
觸目愁腸斷。
砌下落梅如雪亂，
拂了一身還滿。

雁來音訊無憑，
路遙歸夢難成。
離恨恰似春草，
更行更遠還生。

Half of the Spring

(To the tune of Qingpingyue)

LI YU (937–978)

half of the spring has gone
since we parted.
Everywhere I look,
I see a heart-breaking scene:
Plum blossoms keep on falling,
falling to the steps like swirling snow.
Hardly have I brushed them off
when I am all covered in white again.

Wild geese come, carrying no message
from you—the distance too far
for me to travel along
even in a dream.
Anguish of separation is like spring grass:
the farther you go, the more it grows.

柳枝詞

李煜 (937–978)

風情漸老見春羞,
到處芳魂感舊游。
多謝長條似相識,
强垂烟穗拂人頭。

82

The Breeze of Passion

(To the tune of Liuzhici)

LI YU (937–978)

No longer young against the breeze
of passion, now, she is shy
with the splendor of the spring, everywhere,
everywhere petals fall, reminding her
of the people who used to go out
with her.

Thanks
to the long willow shoot that bends
itself for her, she succumbs
to the mist-like tassel caressing
her face, as if touched
by an old companion.

相見歡

李煜(937–978)

無言獨上西樓，
月如鈎。
寂寞梧桐深院鎖清秋。

剪不斷，
理還亂，
是離愁，
別是一番滋味在心頭。

Sorrow of Separation
(*To the tune of Xiangjianhuan*)

LI YU (937–978)

Silent, solitary,

I step up the western tower.

The moon appears like a hook.

The lone parasol tree locks the clear autumn

in the deep courtyard.

What cannot be cut,

nor raveled,

is the sorrow of separation:

Nothing tastes like that to the heart.

一斛珠

李煜（937-978）

曉妝初過，
沉檀輕注些兒個。
向人微露丁香顆，
一曲清歌，
暫引櫻桃破。

羅袖裛殘殷色可，
杯深漸被香醪涴。
繡床斜憑嬌無那，
爛嚼紅茸，
笑向檀郎唾。

A Scarlet Thread

(To the tune of Yixiezhu)

LI YU (937–978)

A finishing touch
to her morning make-up,
she applies a drop of sandalwood rouge
at the corner of her mouth,
a smile revealing her white teeth
like budding lilac, a fresh song popping
a cherry of her red lips.

The musk slightly faint,
her red satin sleeves wet with the sweet wine
filled and refilled in her cup, reclining
on the embroidered bed, infinitely
alluring, chewing a scarlet thread,
she spits it, smiling, at his face.

相見歡

李煜 (937-978)

林花謝了春紅。
太匆匆!
無奈朝來寒雨晚來風。

胭脂泪,
相留醉,
幾時重?
自是人生長恨水長東!

The Rouge-Colored Tear

(To the tune of Wuyeti)

LI YU (937–978)

Soon, the spring splendor fades
from the flowers
in the woods, too soon.
There's no stopping the chill rain at dawn,
or the shrill wind at night.

The memories of the rouge-colored
tears, of the stays overnight
amid cups . . .
When will all that happen again?
Life is long in sadness
as water keeps flowing and flowing east.

浪淘沙

李煜(937–978)

簾外雨潺潺，
春意闌珊。
羅衾不耐五更寒.
夢裏不知身是客，
一晌貪歡。

獨自莫憑闌，
無限江山。
別時容易見時難.
落花流水春去也，
天上人間。

A Changed World

(*To the tune of Langtaosha*)

LI YU (937–978)

Beyond the curtain, the rain keeps pattering,
the spring on the decline.
The satin quilt is not enough
to resist the dawn chill.
Forgetting I'm far, far away from home,
in the dream, I was carried away
with a short spell of pleasure.

Don't lean on the railing, alone—
the boundless view of rivers and mountains.
It's easy to leave, but hard to see again.
The water flows, flowers fall, and the spring fades.
It's a changed world.

虞美人

李煜 (937-978)

春花秋月何時了,
往事知多少?
小樓昨夜又東風,
故國不堪回首月明中。

雕欄玉砌應猶在,
只是朱顏改。
問君能有幾多愁,
恰似一江春水向東流。

Spring Flower and Autumn Moon

(To the tune of Yumeiren)

LI YU (937–978)

When will the endless cycle

of the spring flower and the autumn moon

come to an end?

How much remembrance of the things past

does a heart know?

Last night, in the attic revisited

by the eastern wind,

it was unbearable to look

toward home in the fair moonlight.

The carved rails and the marble steps must remain

unchanged, but not her beauty.

How much sorrow do I have?

It is like the spring flood of a long river flowing east!

雨霖鈴

柳永 (987-1053)

寒蟬淒切，
對長亭晚，
驟雨初歇。
都門帳飲無緒，
留戀處，
蘭舟催發。
執手相看淚眼，
竟無語凝噎。
念去去，
千裏煙波，
暮靄沉沉楚天闊。

Cicadas Chill, Shrill

(To the tune of Yulinling)

LIU YONG (987–1053)

Cicadas screech chill,
shrill, after a sudden shower.
By the roadside pavilion
in the evening, we are parting
outside the city gate, no mood
for the farewell drink, no strength
to tear ourselves apart, when
the magnolia boat urges me to board.
We gaze into each other's eyes
in tears, hand holding
hand, all our words choked.
I'm sailing out, for thousands of miles
along the mist-enveloped waves,
the somber dusk haze
deepening against the boundless southern sky.

多情自古傷離別,
更那堪,
冷落清秋節!
今宵酒醒何處?
楊柳岸,
曉風殘月。
此去經年,
應是良辰好景虛設。
便縱有千種風情,
更與何人說?

It's been hard for lovers to part

since time immemorial.

How much more so

at this cold, deserted autumn!

Tonight, where shall I find

myself, waking from a hangover—

against the riverbank lined with weeping willows

the moon sinking, and the dawn rising

on a breeze? Year

after year, I will be far away from you.

All these beautiful scenes are unfolding,

but to no avail.

Oh, to whom can I speak

of this ineffably enchanting landscape?

浣溪沙

晏殊 (991-1055)

一曲新詞酒一杯,
去年天氣舊亭臺。
夕陽西下幾時回?

無可奈何花落去,
似曾相識燕歸來。
小園香徑獨徘徊。

Helpless That the Flowers Fall

(To the tune of Huanqisha)

YAN SHU (991–1055)

A new poem over a cup of wine,
the last year's weather, the old pavilion.
The sun is setting in the west—
how many times?

Helpless that flowers fall.
Swallows return, seemingly no strangers.
I wander along the sweet-scented trail
in the small garden, alone.

卜算子

李之儀 (?-1117)

我住長江頭，
君住長江尾。
日日思君不見君，
共飲長江水。

此水幾時休，
此恨何時已。
只願君心似我心，
定不負相思意。

Drink from the Same River

Li Zhiyi (?-d.1117)

I live at the upper end of the Yangtze River.
You live at the low end of the Yangtze River.
I miss you, day in, day out.
We drink from the same river.

When will the water stop flowing?
When will the pain cease hurting?
If only your heart is like mine,
there's no letting each other down!

寄内

孔平仲（1050年間）

試說途中景，
方知別后心：
行人日幕少，
風雪亂山深。

Letter to Wife

Kong Pingchong (around 1050)

Let me try to describe
to you a scene
of the journey, and you will see
what has informed my heart
since our parting:
the sun setting,
few stragglers trudging,
hills tangled deep
in the wind and snow.

生查子

歐陽修(1007–1072)

去年元夜時，
花市燈如畫。
月上柳梢頭，
人約黃昏后。

今年元夜時，
月與燈依舊，
不見去年人，
淚濕春衫袖。

Lantern Festival

(To the tune of Shengchazi)

OUYANG XIU (1007–1072)

At the Lantern Festival last year,
The fair was lit like a bright day.
In the night, he met me here,
the moon topping the willow tree.

At the Lantern Festival this year,
The same lanterns, the same moon,
where is the man I met last year?
My spring sleeves are tear-soaked.

木蘭花

歐陽修（1007-1072）

別后不知君遠近，
觸目淒涼多少悶！
漸行漸遠漸無書，
水闊魚沉何處問？

夜深風竹敲秋韵，
萬葉千聲皆是恨。
故欹單枕夢中尋，
夢又不成燈又燼。

How far You Have Traveled

(To the tune of Mulanhua)

OUYANG XIU (1007–1072)

How far you have traveled,
I don't know. Whatever I look at
fills my heart with melancholy.
The farther you go, the fewer
your letters for me. The expanse
of the water so wide, no fish
visible in sight, where and whom
can I ask for your news?

The night deep, the bamboo grooves
beat an autumn melody
in the wind, thousands of leaves
sighing with distress.
Against the solitary pillow, I try
to look for you in a dream,
which does not come
with the wick burning to ashes.

臨江仙

晏幾道(1030-1106)

夢后樓臺高鎖，
酒醒簾幕低垂。
去年春恨却來時。
落花人獨立，
微雨燕雙飛。

記得小蘋初見，
兩重心字羅衣。
琵琶弦上説相思。
當時明月在，
曾照彩雲歸。

Returning like a Radiant Cloud

(To the tune of Linjiangxian)

YAN JIDAO (1030–1106)

Waking with a hangover, I look up
to see the high balcony door
locked, the curtain
hung low. Last spring,
the sorrow of separation new,
long, long I stood,
alone,
amidst all the falling petals:
A pair of swallows fluttered
in the drizzle.

I still remember how
Xiao Ping appeared the first time,
in her silken clothes embroidered
with a double character of *heart*,
pouring out her passion
on the strings of a Pipa.
The bright moon illuminated her returning
like a radiant cloud.

鷓鴣天

晏幾道 (1030–1106)

彩袖殷勤捧玉鐘，
當年拚却醉顏紅。
舞低楊柳樓心月，
歌盡桃花扇影風。

從別后，
憶相逢，
幾回魂夢與君同！
今宵剩把銀缸照，
猶恐相逢是夢中。

110

Florid Sleeves
(To the tune of Zhegutian)

YAN JIDAO (1048–1113)

Holding the jade cup to you,
with my arms reaching
out of the florid sleeves,
I was so happy drinking with you,
heedless of my flushed cheeks, dancing
with the moon sinking
in the willow trees, singing
until I was too tired
to wave the fan that unfolds
a peach blossom.

How I have since missed you,
dreaming of meeting you again and again.

Tonight, I keep turning the silver lamp
to your face. Oh, we are really together,
yet I'm afraid we're meeting
in a recurring dream.

蝶戀花

晏幾道(1030-1106)

醉別西樓醒不記。
春夢秋雲，
聚散真容易。
斜月半窗還少睡，
畫屏閑展吳山翠。

衣上酒痕詩裏字，
點點行行，
總是淒涼意。
紅燭自憐無好計，
夜寒空替人垂泪。

The West Building

(To the tune of Dielianhua)

YAN JIDAO (1030–1106)

What happened in the parting, in my cups
in the west building, I cannot remember, waking
from a drunk sleep.
Dreams in the spring,
Clouds in the autumn.
It is easy to meet, and to part too.
The moon slanting through the window,
I lie sleepless. The painted screen
unfolds, at its leisure,
the verdant southern mountains.

The wine-stains on the clothes,
the words in the poem, line
upon line, drop after drop,
all speak of melancholy.
Even the red candle feels helpless,
in the cold night, shedding tears
for me, in vain.

卜算子

王觀（1050 年間）

水是眼波橫，
山是眉峰聚。
欲問行人去哪邊？
眉眼盈盈處。

才始送春歸，
又送君歸去。
若到江南趕上春，
千萬和春住！

Farewell to a Friend
(To the tune of Busuanzi)
WANG GUAN (AROUND 1050)

Water flows in the rippling
of her eyes.
              Mountains rise
in the knitting of her brows.
So where is a traveler going to visit?
The enchanting landscape
of her eyes and brows.

I have just seen off Spring.
Now you, too, are leaving.
When you catch up with Spring
south of the river, make sure
to stay with her.

江城子

蘇軾 (1036–1101)

十年生死兩茫茫,
不思量,
自難忘。
千裏孤墳,
無處話淒凉。
縱使相逢應不識:
塵滿面,
鬢如霜。

夜來幽夢忽還鄉,
小軒窗,
正梳妝。
相顧無言,
惟有淚千行。
料得年年腸斷處,
明月夜,
短松崗。

Ten Years

(To the tune of Jiangchengzi)

SU SHI (1036–1101)

Ten years, ten years:
> *nothingness*

between life and death.
I try not to think, but I forget not.
The solitary grave, thousands
of miles away. Where else can I tell
the sorrow of my heart?
You would not recognize me if we met:
my face dust-covered,
my temples frost white.

Last night, the dream brought me back
to our old home, where,
by the small window,
you were applying your make-up.
We gazed at each other
in silence, our tears flowing.
It must be the same heart-breaking scene, year after year,
the bright moon night, the short pine hill.

賀新郎

蘇軾 (1036-1101)

乳燕飛華屋，
悄無人，桐陰轉午，
晚凉新浴。
手弄生綃白團扇，
扇手一時似玉。
漸困倚，孤眠清熟。
簾外誰來推綉户？
枉教人夢斷瑶臺曲。
又却是風敲竹。

The Small Swallow

(To the tune of Hexinglang)

SU SHI (1037–1101)

The small swallows fly down
to the magnificent house
in silent solitude.
The shadow of the locust tree keeps
moving into the afternoon.
After a fresh bath,
in the cool evening breeze
of the early summer, she waves
a white silk fan
in her hand, both jade-exquisite.
Feeling gradually drowsy, she
drifts into a sleep against the tired pillow.
Outside the curtain, who is knocking
at the door? Her dream
of the celestial palace is gone.
Oh it is the wind knocking at the bamboo.

石榴半吐紅巾蹙，
待浮花浪蕊都盡，
伴君幽獨。
濃艷一枝細看取，
芳心千重似束。
又恐被西風驚綠。
若待得君來向此，
花前對酒不忍觸。
共粉淚兩簌簌。

120

Waiting for the fall
of the peach and apricot blossoms,
a budding pomegranate flower presents
itself like a rumpled scarlet scarf
to keep her company.
A blaze of the scarlet bloom, she
studies, petal upon petal
as if heavy with thoughts,
worrying about the greenness soon to be lost
in an autumn wind.

Some day, when she sees him again,
holding a cup by the flower,
she will not have the heart to touch it,
the petals falling, her tears falling.

永遇樂

蘇軾 (1036-1101)

明月如霜，
好風如水，
清景無限。
曲港跳魚，
圓荷瀉露，
寂寞無人見。
紞如三鼓，
鏗然一葉，
黯黯夢雲驚斷。
夜茫茫，
重尋無處，
覺來小園行遍。

Swallow Pavilion

(*To the tune of Yongyule*)

SU SHI (1037–1101)

The moon bright as frost,
the breeze soft as water,
a scene of ineffable beauty,
fishes jumping in a curving pond,
dew rolling around the locust leaves,
all of these lies in solitude
visible to no one.

At the third watch struck by night watchman,
the leaves rustle in a high pitch,
dispelling the somber dream clouds
by surprise. The night advanced, I awake,
no way to renew my walk
along the old garden:
a tired traveler stranded at the end of the world,
gazing homeward, heartbroken.

天涯倦客，
山中歸路，
望斷故國心眼。
燕子樓空，
佳人何在？
空鎖樓中燕。
古今如夢，
何曾夢覺，
但有舊歡新怨。
异時對，
黄樓夜景，
爲余浩嘆。

The Swallow Pavilion* is deserted.

Where is the beauty?

Swallows alone are locked inside, for no purpose.

It is nothing but a dream,

in the past, or at present.

Who ever wakes out of the dream?

There is only a never-ending cycle

of old joy, and new grief.

Some day, some one else,

in view of the yellow tower at night,

may sigh deeply for me.

*Swallow Pavilion was known because Guan Panpan, a celebrated courtesan, had once lived in it.

卜算子

蘇軾 (1036-1101)

缺月挂疏桐，
漏斷人初静。
時見幽人獨往來，
飄渺孤鴻影。

驚起却回頭，
有恨無人省。
揀盡寒枝不肯栖，
楓落吴江冷。

Lines Written in Dinghui Temple, Huangzhou

(To the tune of Bosuanzi)

SU SHI (1037–1101)

The waning moon hangs on the sparse tung twigs,
the night deep, silent.
An apparition of a solitary wild goose
moves like a hermit.

Startled, it turns back,
its sorrow unknown to others.
Trying each of the chilly boughs,
it chooses not to perch.
Freezing, the maple leaves fall
over the Wu River.

*In 1082, Su Shi lived in Huangzhou in exile.

洞仙歌

蘇軾(1036–1101)

冰肌玉骨，
自清凉無汗。
水殿風來暗香滿。
繡簾開，
一點明月窺人：
人未寢，
散枕釵橫鬢亂。

起來攜素手，
庭户無聲，
時見疏星渡河漢。
試問夜如何？
夜已三更，

Night Song

(To the tune Tongxiange)

Su Shi (1036–11021)

Immaculate as white jade, as crystal ice,
your body lies cool, sweatless, in the water palace
full of the subtle fragrance
brought in by a breeze.
The curtain pulled aside,
a speck of the bright moon peeps in
to find you sleepless, your hair
disheveled, a hairpin
dropped against the pillow.

Taking your slender hand, we rise
to stand in the silent courtyard.
Occasionally, a stray star is seen shooting
across the Milky Way.
"How advanced is the night?"

金波淡
玉繩低轉。
但屈指西風幾時來，
又不道流年暗中偷換。

130

"The night watchman has struck the third watch."
Golden waves of the moonlight fading,
a jade handle of the Dipper lowering,
we calculate with our fingers
when the west wind will come,
unaware of time flowing away like a river in the dark.

鵲橋仙

秦觀 (1048-1113)

纖雲弄巧，
飛星傳恨，
銀漢迢迢暗度。
金風玉露一相逢，
便勝却人間無數。

柔情似水，
佳期如夢，
忍顧鵲橋歸路？
兩情若是久長時，
又豈在朝朝暮暮！

Meeting across the Milky Way

(*To the tune of Queqiaoxian*)

QIN GUAN (1049–1100)

Through the varying shapes of the delicate clouds,
the sad message of the shooting stars,
a silent journey across the Milky Way,
one meeting of the Cowherd and Weaver
amidst the golden autumn wind and jade-glistening dew,
eclipses the countless meetings
in the mundane world.

The feelings soft as water,
the ecstatic moment unreal as a dream,
how can one have the heart to go back
on the bridge made of magpies?
If the two hearts are united forever,
why do the two persons need to stay
together—day after day,
night after night?

*According to a Chinese legend, two constellations the Cowherd and
Weaver, separated by the Milky Way, are allowed to meet across a
bridge formed by the winds magpies once a year on the seventh day of
the seventh month in the Chinese lunar calendar.

少年游

周邦彦 (1057–1121)

并刀如水，
吳鹽勝雪，
纖手破新橙。
錦幄初溫，
獸香不斷，
相對坐調笙。

低聲問：向誰行宿?
城上已三更。
馬滑霜濃，
不如休去，
直是少人行。

Joy of the Young
(To the tune of Shaonianyou)

ZHOU BANGYAN (1057–1121)

The knife from Bing sharp as water,
the salt from Wu white as snow,
she cuts for him a fresh orange
in her slender fingers.
Behind the newly warmed brocade curtain,
the incense incessantly rising
from the animal-shaped burner,
they sit opposite each other,
tuning up their reed pipe instruments.

Softly she inquires:
"Where are you going to spend the night?
It's the third watch on the city wall,
the frost thick, the road too slippery
for the horse. Don't leave.
Really, few people walk outside."

蝶戀花

周邦彥 (1057-1121)

月皎驚烏栖不定，
更漏將殘，
轆轤牽金井。
喚起兩眸清炯炯，
泪花落枕紅綿冷。

執手霜風吹鬢影，
去意徊徨，
別語愁難聽。
樓上欄杆橫鬥柄，
露寒人遠雞相應。

The Birds Restless
(*To the tune of Dielianhua*)

ZHOU BANGYAN (1057–1121)

The pale moonlight startles the birds,
the night drawing to an end.
Now comes the sound of the windlass rising
out of the well, bringing up the light
in your eyes, clear and bright,
your rouge-smeared tears
cold on the soft pillow.

Holding your hand, I feel the frosty wind
rumpling your hair at the temples.
It's so hard to tear myself away,
to listen to the heartrending words
at parting. High overhead,
the Plough appears across the skies.
The dewdrops chilly, the footsteps distant,
in correspondence to the crowing cock.

玉樓春

周邦彥(1057-1121)

桃溪不作從容住，
秋藕絕來無續處。
當時相候赤闌橋，
今日獨尋黃葉路。

烟中列岫青無數，
雁背夕陽紅欲暮。
人如風后入江雲，
情似雨余粘地絮。

Broken Lotus Root
(*To the tune of Yulouchun*)
ZHOU BANGYAN (1057–1121)

Young, we threw away the pastoral years.
Now like a broken lotus root it is,
impossible to join the present
and the past. Then,
we waited for each other,
standing by the vermilion-railed bridge.
Today, I search for the traces, in vain,
along the deserted path buried under yellow leaves.

Through the mist, all the peaks
seem to be highlighting the blue.
Setting on the back of a wild goose,
the sun turns into a dark red.

You left, like a cloud drifting away,
across the river. The memory of
our passion is like a willow catkin
stuck to the ground, after the rain.

采桑子

吕本中（1084–1145）

恨君不似江樓月，
南北東西。
南北東西，
只有相隨無別離。

恨君却似江樓月，
暫滿還虧。
暫滿還虧，
待得團圓是幾時？

Not Like the Moon
(*To the tune of Caisangzi*)
LÜ BENZHONG (1084–1145)

A pity—you are not like the moon

above the river pavilion:

east, west, north, south,

east, west, north, south . . .

following me everywhere

without separation.

A pity—you are like the moon

above the river pavilion:

waxing and waning,

waxing and waning . . .

when will be the full circle

of our union?

醉花陰

李清照（1084-1151）

薄霧濃雲愁永晝，
瑞腦消金獸。
佳節又重陽，
玉枕紗厨，
半夜涼初透。

東籬把酒黃昏后，
有暗香盈袖。
莫道不消魂，
簾卷西風，
人比黃花瘦。

Thinner Than the Chrysanthemum

(To the tune of Zhuihuayin)

LI QINGZHAO (1084–1151)

The mist thin, the clouds thick, melancholy
all day long.
The incense keeps burning
in the golden animal-shaped censer.
Again comes the festival of Chongyang.
The jade pillow and the gauze valance
feel chilly at midnight.

I hold a cup by the eastern fence
in the evening, the faint fragrance
filling my sleeves. Do not say
the scene is not heart-breaking.
The curtain lifted by the western wind
reveals me
thinner than the chrysanthemum.

沈園二首

陸游（1125-1210）

城上斜陽畫角哀，
沈園非復舊池臺。
傷心橋下春波綠，
曾是驚鴻照影來。

The Shen Garden*

Lu You (1125–1210)

I

The sun is sinking behind the city wall
to the sad notes of a shining bugle.
In the Shen Garden,
the pond and the pavilion appear
no longer to be the same,
except the heart-breaking spring ripples
still so green under the bridge,
the ripples that reflected her arrival
light-footed, in such beauty
as would shame a wild goose into fleeing.

夢斷香銷四十年，
沈園柳老不吹綿。
此身行作稽山土，
猶弔遺踪一泫然。

II

It's forty years since we last met,

the dream broken, the scent vanished,

in the Shen Garden, the aged willows

produce no more catkins.

I'm old, already turning into the dust

of Mount Ji, when I shed a drop of tear

at this old scene.

*The two poems are autobiographical. In his youth, Lu fell in love with
his cousin, Tang, and married her. Due to the opposition from his
mother, they were forced to divorce. When he was seventy-five, he
revisited the garden where they had met, and wrote the two poems.

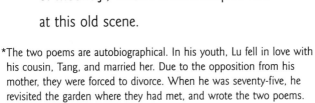

念奴嬌　書東流村壁

辛弃疾 (1140-1207)

野棠花落，
又匆匆過了，
清明時節。
劃地東風欺客夢，
一枕雲屏寒怯。
曲岸持觴，
垂楊系馬，
此地曾輕別。
樓空人去，
舊游飛燕能説.

Lines Written on a Wall of Dongliu Village

(To the tune of Niannujiao)

X<small>IN</small> Q<small>IJI</small> (1140–1207)

Wild pear blossoms start falling again,

so soon, the Qingming festival over.

The cruel eastern wind, for no reason,

interrupts a traveler's dream.

I awake, the brocade curtain

devastatingly cold. Once,

she held the drink to me

on the winding river bank,

and we bade farewell to each other

under a weeping willow tree

with my horse tethered to it.

Now, the pavilion deserted,

there is no trace of her,

only the swallows twittering about bygones.

聞道綺陌東頭，
行人曾見，
簾底纖纖月。
舊恨春江流不盡，
新恨雲山千疊。
料得明朝，
尊前重見，
鏡裏花難折。
也應驚問：
近來多少華發？

She's been seen, people say,
east of the bustling thoroughfare,
behind the curtain, still as graceful
as the new moon. Old regrets
run like the endless spring water. New griefs
pile up like the clouds over the mountains.
If we were going to meet again,
at a banquet, to tell her all this
would be as impossible
as to pluck the flower from a mirror.
She would say, perhaps,
How white you hair has grown!

暗香

姜夔 (1155-1221)

舊時月色,
算幾番照我
梅邊吹笛?
喚起玉人,
不管清寒與攀摘。
何遜而今漸老,
都忘却春風詞筆。
但怪得竹外疏花
香冷入瑶席。

Hidden Fragrance

(To the tune of Anxiang)

JIANG KUI (1155–1221)

ow often did the moon of old
illuminate me playing a bamboo flute
under a plum tree?
I would wake her, a beauty of jade,
to pluck a blossoming sprig
in spite of the chilly air.

Now no longer young, forgetting
about the spring breeze flowing
out of my brush pen,
I wonder how the cold fragrance,
coming from the sparse petals, beyond the
     bamboo groove,
disturbs the wine in my cup.

江國正寂寞。
嘆寄與路遙,
夜雪初積。
翠尊易泣,
紅萼無言耿相憶。
長記曾攜手處,
千樹壓西湖寒碧。
又片片吹盡也,
幾時見得?

154

The south of Yangtze lies in solitude.

The branches weighed down

by the night's snow, I try to break a sprig,

in vain, for the one now far, far away.

The clear liquor seems to be sobbing

in an emerald goblet, the red blossoms

silent, yet stubborn in my memory.

Long I remember where we stood, hand in hand,

viewing thousands of trees reflecting

on the cold green West Lake.

All are soon blown out of sight,

petals after petals.

When can I see her again?

虞美人

蔣捷 （1250年間）

少年聽雨歌樓上，
紅燭昏羅帳。
壯年聽雨客舟中，
江闊雲低，
斷雁叫西風。

而今聽雨僧廬下，
鬢已星星也。
悲歡離合總無情，
一任階前點滴到天明。

Listen to the Rain

(To the tune of Yu Meiren)

JIANG JIE (AROUND 1250)

Young, I listened to the rain
in the houses of pleasure,
the silk valence silhouetted
against a red candle.
Middle-aged, I listened to the rain
in a boat, the stream wide, the clouds low,
a lost wild goose wailing
in the western wind.

Now I listen to the rain
under a temple's eaves, my hair starred
in silver. People meet
in joy, part in grief,
but what do I care?
Let the rain drip onto the steps,
drop after drop till dawn.

寄子昂君墨竹

管道升（1250年間）

夫君去日竹初栽，
竹已成林君末來。
玉貌一衰難再好，
不如花落又花開。

On a Painting of the Bamboo to Zi'an*

GUAN DAOSHENG (AROUND 1250)

The day that you left,

we planted the bamboo roots.

Now the tall bamboo grove sways

in the wind, there's still no sign

of your coming back.

Growing old, I won't blossom

into a jade-like beauty for one more time,

not like the flowers which, after falling,

will burgeon afresh.

*Guan's husband Zhao Zi'ang was a high official as well as a celebrated
painter and calligrapher in the Song dynasty. This was a poem Guan
wrote on a painting of bamboo sent to her husband.

我儂詞

管道升（1250年間）

你儂我儂，
忒煞情多，
情多處熱似火！
把一塊泥，
捏一個你，
塑一個我。
將咱兩個，
一齊打破，
用水調和，
再捏一個你，
再塑一個我。
我泥中有你，
你泥中有我！

You and I

GUAN DAOSHENG (AROUND 1250)

You and I are so crazy
about each other,
as hot as a potter's fire.
Out of the same chunk
of clay, shape a you,
shape a me. Crush us
both into clay again, mix
it with water, reshape
a you, reshape a me.
So, I have you in my body,
and you'll have me forever in yours, too.

天净沙

馬致遠 (1250-1324)

枯藤老樹昏鴉，
小橋流水人家，
古道西風瘦馬。

夕陽西下，
斷腸人在天涯。

Autumn Thought

(To the tune of Tianjingsha)

MA ZHIYUAN (1250–1321)

Withered vines, old trees, crows at dusk,
a small bridge over the flowing water, a few houses,
an ancient path, the west wind, a lean horse,
and the sun setting . . .
A heart-broken traveler at the end of the world.

越歌

宋濂(1300年間)

戀郎思郎非一朝,
好似并州花剪刀。
一股在南一股北,
何時裁得合歡袍?

Song of Yue

SONG LIAN (AROUND 1300)

It is not just a day or a night that I have
    missed you, Lord.
It is like a broken pair
of Bingzhou scissors—
one blade is far in the south, and the other, far
in the north.
When can the pair
be joined to cut out a wedding gown?

蝶戀花

納蘭性德(1655-1685)

辛苦最憐天上月，
一昔如環，
昔昔都成缺。
若似月輪終皎潔，
不辭冰雪爲卿熱。

無那塵緣容易絕，
燕子依然，
軟踏簾鈎說。
唱罷秋墳愁未歇，
春叢認取雙栖蝶。

Piteous the Moon
(To the tune of Dielianhua)

NALAN XINDE (1655–1685)

So piteous the moon seems:
a full circle keeps waning,
waning into half a circle, and then
all over again, night after night.
If only you could recover likewise,
from the half to the full,
your body, cold as ice, as snow,
would be brought to life
by the warmth of mine.

Irrecoverably, you left me.
The swallows twitter lovingly, as before,
on the soft valance hooks.
It does not alleviate my agony
to sing through the "Autumn Elegies."
Oh that we could be a pair of butterflies
flying amidst the spring flowers,
in the next life.

綺懷

黃景仁(1749-1783)

幾回花下坐吹簫，
銀漢紅墻入望遙。
似此星辰非昨夜，
爲誰風露立中宵。

纏綿思盡抽殘繭，
宛轉心傷剩后蕉。
三五年時三五月，
可憐杯酒不曾消。

Reverie

HUANG JINGREN (1749–1783)

How many times have I played the
    bamboo flute
amidst the flowers, gazing at the red walls
below the silver skies?
What a starry night this is,
but not that night, long ago, lost.
For whom do I find myself standing here,
against the wind and the frost,
deep in the night?

Feeling never-ending,
spun out of a spent silkworm cocoon,
my heart trembles like a banana palm tree
stripped of all the leaves.
At fifteen, she watched the moon with me
on the fifteenth night of the month,
the memory of which fails
to drown in a cup of wine.

About the Author

Q_JIU XIAOLONG was born in China. He started writing and translating poetry in Chinese in the early 1980s and was selected for membership in the Chinese Writers Association. He moved to the United States in 1989 and received his master's and doctorate degrees in comparative literature from Washington University in St. Louis. For his writing in English, Xiaolong has received the Missouri Biennial Award and the Prairie Schooner Reader's Choice Award, as well as a Yaddo and a Ford fellowship. His novel *Death of a Red Heroine* was nominated for Edgar and Barry awards and received the Anthony Award. He since has published a second novel, *A Loyal Character Dancer*. Xiaolong lives in St. Louis with his wife and daughter.

From Hippocrene's Chinese Library

Beginner's Chinese

This introduction to Mandarin Chinese is designed for those with little or no prior experience in the language. Beginning with an in-depth look at the language prominent features, including Chinese phonetics and the written language, it provides the most basic and crucial words and patterns to enable the student to immediately communicate in Chinese. Each lesson consists of the following: Basic sentence patterns; dialogues to illustrate the use of these patterns; vocabulary and expressions; language points; exercises; and cultural insights about the topic of each lesson. Upon completion of this course, the student will have learned 90 basic sentence patterns, 300 characters, basic grammar, and communicative skills.

173 pages • 5½ x 8½ • 0-7818-0566-X • $14.95pb • W • (690)

Chinese-English Frequency Dictionary: A Study Guide to Mandarin Chinese's 500 Most Frequently Used Words

Functioning as both a traditional dictionary and a study guide, this list of the 500 most frequently used words (characters) of Mandarin Chinese offers the English-speaking student of Chinese an essential source of vocabulary and a detailed reference to the world's most widely spoken language. Presented in order of frequency, each entry includes the Chinese character with pinyin transcription, meaning, explanations of usage with examples, and a selection of words and expressions that have the entry word as the first element. Two indices also list the 500 words according to frequency and alphabetical order.

500 entries • 240 pages • 5½ x 8½ • 0-7818-0842-1 • $16.95pb • W • (277)

China: An Illustrated History

This concise, illustrated volume offers the reader a panoramic view of this remarkable land, from antiquity to the twenty-first century. Among other topics, it explores sources of Chinese thought, cornerstones of Chinese political, religious and economic institutions, and the cohesive ties that have bound China as a nation for thousands of years.

142 pages • 50 illustrations • 5 x 7 • 0-7818-0821-9 • $14.95hc • W • (542)

Hippocrene Children's Illustrated Chinese (Mandarin) Dictionary
English-Chinese/Chinese-English

Designed to be a child's first foreign language dictionary, for ages 5–10, each entry is accompanied by a large illustration, the English word and its equivalent, along with commonsense phonetic pronunciation. Entries include people, animals, colors, numbers and objects that children encounter and use every day.

94 pages • 500 entries/illus. • 8½ x 11 • 0-7818-0848-0 • $11.95pb • W • (662)

Hippocrene's Bilingual Love Poetry Library

African
0-7818-0483-3 • $11.95hc
Arabic
0-7818-0395-0 • $11.95hc
Czech
0-7818-0571-6 • $11.95hc
Finnish
0-7818-0397-7 • $11.95hc
French
0-7818-0307-1 • $11.95hc
French, Volume 2
0-7818-0930-4 • $11.95hc
German
0-7818-0296-2 • $11.95hc
Hungarian
0-7818-0477-9 • $11.95hc
Indian
0-7818-0670-4 • $11.95hc
Irish
0-7818-0644-5 • $11.95hc
Irish cassettes
0-7818-0748-4 • $12.95
Italian
0-7818-0352-7 • $11.95hc
Italian cassettes
0-7818-0366-7 • $12.95

Jewish
0-7818-0308-X • $11.95hc
Mexican
0-7818-0985-1 • $11.95hc
Polish
0-7818-0297-0 • $11.95hc
Polish
0-7818-0969-X • $11.95hc
Adam Mickiewicz in Polish and English
0-7818-0652-6 • $11.95hc
Roman
0-7818-0309-8 • $11.95hc
Russian
0-7818-0298-9 • $11.95hc
Russian cassettes
0-7818-0364-0 • $12.95
Spanish
0-7818-0358-6 • $11.95hc
Spanish cassettes
0-7818-0365-9 • $12.95
Ukrainian
0-7818-0517-1 • $11.95hc

All prices are subject to change without prior notice. To order **Hippocrene Books**, contact your local bookstore, call (718) 454-2366, visit www.hippocrenebooks.com, or write to: Hippocrene Books, 171 Madison Avenue, New York, NY 10016. Please enclose check or money order adding $5.00 shipping (UPS) for the first book and $.50 for each additional title.